50 Simple & Delicious: A Beginner's Guide Recipes

By: Kelly Johnson

Table of Contents

- Scrambled Eggs
- Boiled Eggs
- Fried Eggs
- Omelet
- Avocado Toast
- Peanut Butter & Jelly Sandwich
- Grilled Cheese Sandwich
- BLT Sandwich
- Tuna Salad Sandwich
- Egg Salad Sandwich
- Simple Pancakes
- French Toast
- Oatmeal with Honey & Berries
- Yogurt Parfait
- Banana Smoothie
- Basic Green Salad
- Caesar Salad
- Cucumber & Tomato Salad
- Chicken & Rice Bowl
- Simple Stir-Fry (Chicken & Veggies)
- Pasta with Marinara Sauce
- Spaghetti Aglio e Olio
- Mac and Cheese
- Ramen with Egg
- Baked Potato
- Mashed Potatoes
- Roasted Vegetables
- Grilled Chicken Breast
- Baked Salmon
- Pan-Seared Steak
- Rice & Beans
- Garlic Butter Shrimp
- Simple Chili
- Chicken Noodle Soup
- Tomato Soup

- Vegetable Soup
- Baked Chicken Thighs
- Meatballs
- Sloppy Joes
- Tacos (Beef or Chicken)
- Quesadilla
- Guacamole
- Hummus with Pita
- Fried Rice
- Cheeseburger
- Hot Dog with Toppings
- Baked Apples with Cinnamon
- Chocolate Mug Cake
- Fruit Salad
- No-Bake Peanut Butter Bars

Scrambled Eggs

Ingredients:

- 2 eggs
- 1 tbsp butter or oil
- 2 tbsp milk (optional)
- Salt and pepper to taste

Instructions:

1. Beat eggs with milk, salt, and pepper.
2. Heat butter in a pan over medium-low heat.
3. Pour in eggs and gently stir until soft curds form.
4. Remove from heat while slightly undercooked; they'll finish cooking off the heat.
5. Serve warm.

Boiled Eggs

Ingredients:

- 2 eggs
- Water

Instructions:

1. Place eggs in a pot and cover with water.
2. Bring to a boil, then cover and remove from heat.
   - Soft-boiled: 6–7 minutes
   - Medium-boiled: 9–10 minutes
   - Hard-boiled: 12–14 minutes
3. Transfer eggs to an ice bath and peel when cool.

Fried Eggs

Ingredients:

- 1 egg
- 1 tbsp butter or oil
- Salt and pepper to taste

Instructions:

1. Heat butter in a pan over medium heat.
2. Crack the egg into the pan.
3. Cook until whites are set (for sunny-side-up).
4. For over-easy, flip and cook for 30 seconds more.
5. Season with salt and pepper before serving.

Omelet

Ingredients:

- 2 eggs
- 2 tbsp milk (optional)
- Salt and pepper
- ½ cup fillings (cheese, veggies, ham, etc.)
- 1 tbsp butter

Instructions:

1. Beat eggs with milk, salt, and pepper.
2. Heat butter in a pan over medium heat.
3. Pour eggs into the pan and cook without stirring.
4. Add fillings to one side and fold the omelet over.
5. Cook for another minute, then serve.

Avocado Toast

Ingredients:

- 1 slice of bread
- ½ ripe avocado
- Salt, pepper, and toppings (optional: tomatoes, egg, chili flakes)

Instructions:

1. Toast bread until golden.
2. Mash avocado and spread over toast.
3. Season with salt and pepper, add toppings, and serve.

Peanut Butter & Jelly Sandwich

Ingredients:

- 2 slices of bread
- 2 tbsp peanut butter
- 2 tbsp jelly or jam

Instructions:

1. Spread peanut butter on one slice of bread.
2. Spread jelly on the other slice.
3. Press both slices together and serve.

Grilled Cheese Sandwich

Ingredients:

- 2 slices of bread
- 2 tbsp butter
- 2 slices of cheese (cheddar, American, etc.)

Instructions:

1. Butter one side of each bread slice.
2. Place cheese between the slices, buttered side out.
3. Cook in a pan over medium heat until golden brown on both sides.
4. Serve warm.

BLT Sandwich

Ingredients:

- 2 slices of bread
- 2 slices cooked bacon
- 2 lettuce leaves
- 2 tomato slices
- 1 tbsp mayonnaise

Instructions:

1. Toast the bread.
2. Spread mayonnaise on one side of each slice.
3. Layer bacon, lettuce, and tomato.
4. Top with the second slice of bread and serve.

Tuna Salad Sandwich

Ingredients:

- 1 can tuna, drained
- 2 tbsp mayonnaise
- 1 tbsp chopped celery (optional)
- 1 tsp lemon juice
- Salt and pepper to taste
- 2 slices of bread

Instructions:

1. Mix tuna, mayonnaise, celery, lemon juice, salt, and pepper.
2. Spread onto one slice of bread.
3. Top with the second slice, cut in half, and serve.

Egg Salad Sandwich

Ingredients:

- 2 hard-boiled eggs, chopped
- 2 tbsp mayonnaise
- 1 tsp mustard (optional)
- Salt and pepper to taste
- 2 slices of bread

Instructions:

1. Mix chopped eggs, mayonnaise, mustard, salt, and pepper.
2. Spread onto one slice of bread.
3. Top with the second slice and serve.

Simple Pancakes

Ingredients:

- 1 cup flour
- 1 tbsp sugar
- 1 tsp baking powder
- 1 egg
- ¾ cup milk
- 1 tbsp melted butter

Instructions:

1. Mix flour, sugar, and baking powder in a bowl.
2. In another bowl, whisk egg, milk, and butter.
3. Combine wet and dry ingredients.
4. Heat a pan and pour in batter.
5. Cook until bubbles form, flip, and cook another minute.
6. Serve with syrup or toppings of choice.

French Toast

Ingredients:

- 2 slices of bread
- 1 egg
- ½ cup milk
- 1 tsp cinnamon (optional)
- 1 tbsp butter
- Syrup for serving

Instructions:

1. Whisk egg, milk, and cinnamon.
2. Dip bread into the mixture, coating both sides.
3. Heat butter in a pan and cook bread until golden brown on both sides.
4. Serve warm with syrup.

Oatmeal with Honey & Berries

Ingredients:

- ½ cup rolled oats
- 1 cup milk or water
- 1 tbsp honey
- ¼ cup mixed berries (strawberries, blueberries, raspberries)
- ½ tsp cinnamon (optional)

Instructions:

1. Bring milk or water to a boil.
2. Stir in oats and cook for 5 minutes, stirring occasionally.
3. Remove from heat and mix in honey.
4. Top with berries and cinnamon, then serve.

Yogurt Parfait

Ingredients:

- 1 cup Greek yogurt
- ½ cup granola
- ½ cup mixed berries
- 1 tbsp honey

Instructions:

1. Layer yogurt, granola, and berries in a glass or bowl.
2. Drizzle with honey.
3. Serve immediately.

Banana Smoothie

Ingredients:

- 1 banana
- 1 cup milk (or almond milk)
- ½ cup yogurt (optional)
- 1 tbsp honey (optional)
- Ice cubes (optional)

Instructions:

1. Blend all ingredients until smooth.
2. Pour into a glass and serve immediately.

Basic Green Salad

Ingredients:

- 4 cups mixed greens (lettuce, spinach, arugula)
- ½ cup cherry tomatoes, halved
- ¼ cup sliced cucumber
- ¼ cup shredded carrots
- 2 tbsp olive oil
- 1 tbsp lemon juice or vinegar
- Salt & pepper to taste

Instructions:

1. Toss greens, tomatoes, cucumber, and carrots in a bowl.
2. Drizzle with olive oil and lemon juice.
3. Season with salt and pepper, then serve.

Caesar Salad

Ingredients:

- 4 cups chopped romaine lettuce
- ¼ cup grated Parmesan cheese
- ½ cup croutons
- ¼ cup Caesar dressing

Instructions:

1. Toss lettuce, Parmesan, and croutons in a bowl.
2. Drizzle with dressing and mix well.
3. Serve immediately.

Cucumber & Tomato Salad

Ingredients:

- 1 cucumber, sliced
- 1 cup cherry tomatoes, halved
- ¼ red onion, thinly sliced
- 2 tbsp olive oil
- 1 tbsp lemon juice
- Salt & pepper to taste

Instructions:

1. Mix cucumber, tomatoes, and onion in a bowl.
2. Drizzle with olive oil and lemon juice.
3. Season with salt and pepper, then serve.

Chicken & Rice Bowl

Ingredients:

- 1 cup cooked rice
- 1 chicken breast, grilled and sliced
- ½ cup steamed vegetables (broccoli, carrots, or bell peppers)
- 1 tbsp soy sauce or teriyaki sauce

Instructions:

1. Place cooked rice in a bowl.
2. Top with sliced grilled chicken and steamed vegetables.
3. Drizzle with soy or teriyaki sauce.
4. Serve warm.

Simple Stir-Fry (Chicken & Veggies)

Ingredients:

- 1 chicken breast, sliced
- 1 cup mixed vegetables (bell peppers, carrots, broccoli)
- 2 tbsp soy sauce
- 1 tbsp olive oil
- 1 garlic clove, minced

Instructions:

1. Heat oil in a pan over medium-high heat.
2. Add chicken and cook until golden.
3. Add vegetables and stir-fry for 3–4 minutes.
4. Add soy sauce and garlic, cook for another minute.
5. Serve hot.

Pasta with Marinara Sauce

Ingredients:

- 1 cup pasta
- ½ cup marinara sauce
- 1 tbsp olive oil
- 1 garlic clove, minced
- ¼ tsp red pepper flakes (optional)
- Parmesan cheese (for topping)

Instructions:

1. Cook pasta according to package instructions.
2. In a pan, heat olive oil and sauté garlic until fragrant.
3. Add marinara sauce and simmer for 5 minutes.
4. Toss with cooked pasta and top with Parmesan cheese.

Spaghetti Aglio e Olio

Ingredients:

- 1 cup spaghetti
- 3 tbsp olive oil
- 2 garlic cloves, thinly sliced
- ¼ tsp red pepper flakes
- 1 tbsp chopped parsley
- Salt to taste

Instructions:

1. Cook spaghetti according to package instructions.
2. In a pan, heat olive oil and sauté garlic until golden.
3. Add red pepper flakes and mix.
4. Toss in cooked spaghetti and mix well.
5. Garnish with parsley and serve.

Mac and Cheese

Ingredients:

- 1 cup elbow macaroni
- 1 tbsp butter
- 1 tbsp flour
- ¾ cup milk
- 1 cup shredded cheddar cheese
- Salt & pepper to taste

Instructions:

1. Cook macaroni according to package instructions.
2. In a pan, melt butter and whisk in flour.
3. Gradually add milk, stirring until smooth.
4. Stir in cheese and mix until melted.
5. Combine with pasta and serve.

Ramen with Egg

Ingredients:

- 1 pack instant ramen
- 1 egg
- 2 cups water
- ½ green onion, chopped (optional)

Instructions:

1. Boil water and cook ramen noodles as per package instructions.
2. When noodles are almost done, crack an egg into the pot.
3. Let the egg cook for 2–3 minutes without stirring.
4. Serve hot with green onions on top.

Baked Potato

Ingredients:

- 1 large russet potato
- 1 tbsp olive oil
- ½ tsp salt
- ¼ tsp black pepper
- Optional toppings: butter, sour cream, cheese, chives, bacon bits

Instructions:

1. Preheat oven to 425°F (220°C).
2. Wash and dry the potato, then poke holes with a fork.
3. Rub with olive oil, salt, and pepper.
4. Bake directly on the oven rack for 45–60 minutes until tender.
5. Cut open, add toppings, and serve.

Mashed Potatoes

Ingredients:

- 4 medium potatoes, peeled and cubed
- ¼ cup butter
- ½ cup milk
- Salt & pepper to taste

Instructions:

1. Boil potatoes until fork-tender (about 15 minutes).
2. Drain and mash with butter and milk.
3. Season with salt and pepper.

Roasted Vegetables

Ingredients:

- 2 cups mixed vegetables (carrots, bell peppers, zucchini, etc.)
- 2 tbsp olive oil
- 1 tsp salt
- ½ tsp black pepper
- ½ tsp garlic powder

Instructions:

1. Preheat oven to 400°F (200°C).
2. Toss vegetables with olive oil, salt, pepper, and garlic powder.
3. Spread on a baking sheet and roast for 20–25 minutes, stirring halfway.

Grilled Chicken Breast

Ingredients:

- 2 boneless, skinless chicken breasts
- 1 tbsp olive oil
- ½ tsp salt
- ½ tsp black pepper
- ½ tsp garlic powder
- ½ tsp paprika

Instructions:

1. Preheat grill to medium-high heat.
2. Brush chicken with olive oil and season with spices.
3. Grill for 5–7 minutes per side until fully cooked.

Baked Salmon

Ingredients:

- 2 salmon fillets
- 1 tbsp olive oil
- 1 tbsp lemon juice
- ½ tsp salt
- ½ tsp black pepper
- ½ tsp garlic powder

Instructions:

1. Preheat oven to 400°F (200°C).
2. Place salmon on a baking sheet, drizzle with olive oil and lemon juice, and season with spices.
3. Bake for 12–15 minutes until flaky.

Pan-Seared Steak

Ingredients:

- 1 steak (ribeye, sirloin, or filet mignon)
- 1 tbsp olive oil
- 1 tbsp butter
- 1 garlic clove, crushed
- Salt & pepper to taste

Instructions:

1. Heat olive oil in a skillet over high heat.
2. Season steak with salt and pepper.
3. Sear for 3–4 minutes per side.
4. Add butter and garlic, basting the steak for 1 minute.
5. Rest for 5 minutes before serving.

Rice & Beans

Ingredients:

- 1 cup rice
- 1½ cups water
- 1 can (15 oz) black or kidney beans, drained
- ½ tsp salt
- ½ tsp cumin
- ½ tsp garlic powder

Instructions:

1. Cook rice according to package instructions.
2. Stir in beans, seasonings, and a splash of water.
3. Simmer for 5 minutes, then serve.

Garlic Butter Shrimp

Ingredients:

- ½ lb shrimp, peeled and deveined
- 2 tbsp butter
- 2 garlic cloves, minced
- ½ tsp salt
- ½ tsp paprika
- 1 tbsp lemon juice

Instructions:

1. Melt butter in a skillet over medium heat.
2. Add garlic and cook for 30 seconds.
3. Add shrimp, salt, and paprika. Cook for 2–3 minutes per side.
4. Drizzle with lemon juice and serve.

Simple Chili

Ingredients:

- 1 lb ground beef
- 1 can (15 oz) kidney beans, drained
- 1 can (15 oz) diced tomatoes
- 1 tbsp chili powder
- ½ tsp salt
- ½ tsp cumin
- 1 onion, diced

Instructions:

1. Brown ground beef in a pot over medium heat.
2. Add onion and cook until soft.
3. Stir in beans, tomatoes, and seasonings.
4. Simmer for 20–30 minutes.

Chicken Noodle Soup

Ingredients:

- 1 chicken breast, shredded
- 4 cups chicken broth
- 1 cup egg noodles
- 1 carrot, sliced
- 1 celery stalk, sliced
- 1 garlic clove, minced
- Salt & pepper to taste

Instructions:

1. Boil chicken breast in broth until cooked, then shred.
2. Add carrots, celery, and garlic. Simmer for 10 minutes.
3. Add noodles and cook for 5–7 minutes.

Tomato Soup

Ingredients:

- 1 can (28 oz) crushed tomatoes
- 1 cup vegetable broth
- 1 tbsp olive oil
- 1 garlic clove, minced
- ½ tsp salt
- ½ tsp sugar
- ¼ cup heavy cream (optional)

Instructions:

1. Heat olive oil in a pot and sauté garlic.
2. Add crushed tomatoes, broth, salt, and sugar.
3. Simmer for 15–20 minutes. Blend until smooth.
4. Stir in heavy cream, if using.

Vegetable Soup

Ingredients:

- 4 cups vegetable broth
- 1 cup mixed vegetables (carrots, potatoes, peas, etc.)
- 1 can (15 oz) diced tomatoes
- 1 tsp salt
- ½ tsp black pepper
- ½ tsp dried oregano

Instructions:

1. In a pot, bring broth to a boil.
2. Add vegetables, tomatoes, and seasonings.
3. Simmer for 20–25 minutes until vegetables are tender.

Baked Chicken Thighs

Ingredients:

- 4 bone-in, skin-on chicken thighs
- 1 tbsp olive oil
- 1 tsp salt
- ½ tsp black pepper
- ½ tsp garlic powder
- ½ tsp paprika
- ½ tsp dried thyme

Instructions:

1. Preheat oven to 400°F (200°C).
2. Pat chicken thighs dry with a paper towel.
3. Rub with olive oil and season with salt, pepper, garlic powder, paprika, and thyme.
4. Place on a baking sheet, skin side up.
5. Bake for 35–40 minutes until golden and crispy.

Meatballs

Ingredients:

- 1 lb ground beef or ground turkey
- ½ cup breadcrumbs
- 1 egg
- ½ cup grated Parmesan cheese
- 1 tsp salt
- ½ tsp black pepper
- ½ tsp garlic powder
- ½ tsp dried oregano
- 1 tbsp olive oil (for frying)
- 1 cup marinara sauce (for serving)

Instructions:

1. Preheat oven to 375°F (190°C).
2. In a bowl, mix all ingredients except olive oil and sauce.
3. Roll into small balls.
4. Heat olive oil in a pan and brown meatballs on all sides.
5. Transfer to a baking dish and bake for 15 minutes.
6. Serve with marinara sauce.

Sloppy Joes

Ingredients:

- 1 lb ground beef
- ½ cup ketchup
- 1 tbsp Worcestershire sauce
- 1 tbsp brown sugar
- ½ tsp salt
- ½ tsp black pepper
- ½ tsp garlic powder
- 1 small onion, diced
- 1 tbsp olive oil
- 4 hamburger buns

Instructions:

1. Heat olive oil in a pan over medium heat.
2. Sauté onions until soft, then add ground beef.
3. Cook until browned, then drain excess fat.
4. Stir in ketchup, Worcestershire sauce, brown sugar, salt, pepper, and garlic powder.
5. Simmer for 5–10 minutes.
6. Serve on hamburger buns.

Tacos (Beef or Chicken)

Ingredients:

- 1 lb ground beef or shredded chicken
- 1 tbsp olive oil
- 1 tsp salt
- ½ tsp black pepper
- 1 tsp chili powder
- ½ tsp cumin
- ½ tsp garlic powder
- ½ cup diced onions
- 8 small taco shells
- Optional toppings: shredded lettuce, cheese, salsa, sour cream

Instructions:

1. Heat olive oil in a pan over medium heat.
2. Add onions and cook until soft.
3. Add ground beef or shredded chicken, then season with salt, pepper, chili powder, cumin, and garlic powder.
4. Cook until beef is browned or chicken is heated through.
5. Spoon into taco shells and add toppings.

Quesadilla

Ingredients:

- 2 large flour tortillas
- 1 cup shredded cheese (cheddar, mozzarella, or Monterey Jack)
- ½ cup cooked chicken or beef (optional)
- 1 tbsp butter
- Optional fillings: sautéed onions, bell peppers, mushrooms

Instructions:

1. Heat a skillet over medium heat.
2. Place one tortilla in the pan and sprinkle with cheese and optional fillings.
3. Top with another tortilla and cook for 2–3 minutes per side until golden and crispy.
4. Slice into wedges and serve.

Guacamole

Ingredients:

- 2 ripe avocados
- ½ small red onion, finely diced
- 1 small tomato, diced
- 1 tbsp lime juice
- ½ tsp salt
- ¼ tsp black pepper
- 1 tbsp chopped cilantro (optional)

Instructions:

1. Mash avocados in a bowl.
2. Stir in onion, tomato, lime juice, salt, and pepper.
3. Mix well and serve with chips or tacos.

Hummus with Pita

Ingredients:

- 1 can (15 oz) chickpeas, drained and rinsed
- ¼ cup tahini
- 2 tbsp olive oil
- 2 tbsp lemon juice
- 1 small garlic clove, minced
- ½ tsp salt
- ¼ tsp cumin
- 2–3 tbsp water (as needed)
- 1 tbsp chopped parsley (optional, for garnish)
- 1 tsp paprika (for garnish)
- Pita bread, for serving

Instructions:

1. Blend chickpeas, tahini, olive oil, lemon juice, garlic, salt, and cumin in a food processor.
2. Add water gradually until smooth and creamy.
3. Transfer to a bowl, drizzle with extra olive oil, and garnish with parsley and paprika.
4. Serve with pita bread.

Fried Rice

Ingredients:

- 2 cups cooked rice (preferably day-old)
- 1 tbsp vegetable oil
- ½ cup diced carrots
- ½ cup frozen peas
- 2 eggs, beaten
- 2 tbsp soy sauce
- 1 tsp sesame oil
- 1 green onion, sliced
- 1 clove garlic, minced

Instructions:

1. Heat oil in a pan over medium heat.
2. Add carrots and cook for 2 minutes. Add garlic and peas, stirring for another minute.
3. Push veggies to one side, pour in beaten eggs, and scramble until cooked.
4. Stir in rice and soy sauce, cooking for 2–3 minutes.
5. Drizzle with sesame oil and garnish with green onions.

Cheeseburger

Ingredients:

- 1 lb ground beef
- ½ tsp salt
- ½ tsp black pepper
- ½ tsp garlic powder
- 4 hamburger buns
- 4 slices cheddar cheese
- Lettuce, tomato, pickles, ketchup, and mustard (optional toppings)

Instructions:

1. Preheat a grill or pan to medium-high heat.
2. Form beef into 4 patties and season with salt, pepper, and garlic powder.
3. Cook for 3–4 minutes per side until browned.
4. Place cheese on patties and cook for another minute.
5. Assemble burgers with buns and desired toppings.

Hot Dog with Toppings

Ingredients:

- 4 hot dog buns
- 4 hot dogs
- ¼ cup diced onions
- ¼ cup relish
- ¼ cup shredded cheese
- ¼ cup ketchup and mustard (for topping)

Instructions:

1. Grill or boil hot dogs until heated through.
2. Place hot dogs in buns and add toppings as desired.

Baked Apples with Cinnamon

Ingredients:

- 2 apples, cored and sliced
- 1 tbsp melted butter
- 1 tbsp brown sugar
- ½ tsp cinnamon
- ¼ tsp nutmeg (optional)
- 2 tbsp chopped walnuts or pecans (optional)

Instructions:

1. Preheat oven to 375°F (190°C).
2. Toss apple slices with butter, brown sugar, cinnamon, and nutmeg.
3. Spread in a baking dish and bake for 20–25 minutes until soft.
4. Sprinkle with nuts if desired.

Chocolate Mug Cake

Ingredients:

- 4 tbsp all-purpose flour
- 4 tbsp sugar
- 2 tbsp cocoa powder
- ⅛ tsp baking powder
- 3 tbsp milk
- 2 tbsp vegetable oil
- ¼ tsp vanilla extract

Instructions:

1. Mix all ingredients in a microwave-safe mug.
2. Microwave for 1–1½ minutes until set.
3. Let cool slightly before enjoying.

Fruit Salad

Ingredients:

- 1 cup strawberries, sliced
- 1 cup grapes, halved
- 1 cup pineapple, diced
- 1 cup blueberries
- 1 tbsp honey (optional)
- 1 tbsp lime juice

Instructions:

1. Combine all fruits in a bowl.
2. Drizzle with honey and lime juice.
3. Toss and serve chilled.

No-Bake Peanut Butter Bars

Ingredients:

- 1 cup peanut butter
- ½ cup honey
- 2 cups rolled oats
- ½ cup chocolate chips (optional)

Instructions:

1. In a bowl, mix peanut butter, honey, and oats.
2. Press mixture into a lined baking dish.
3. Melt chocolate chips and spread over the top.
4. Refrigerate for 1 hour, then cut into bars.

www.ingramcontent.com/pod-product-compliance
Lightning Source LLC
LaVergne TN
LVHW081503060526
838201LV00056BA/2905